Writing
Works Wonders

WEB DESIGN *for* AUTHORS

Visionary Series
We Do It With Our Eyes Closed

DR. KATHLEEN P. KING
CHERYL MCNEIL FISHER

TABLE OF CONTENTS

ABOUT THE AUTHORS

DR. KATHLEEN P. KING

Kathy King is an award-winning author and editor who has published over 30 books and 200+ articles and papers. She also founded and edited several journals and book series. She launched her digital media consulting group, Transformation Education, in 1991. While a professor and author, Kathy also has been building websites for her clients since the dawn of the web.

In addition to designing websites and digital platforms, she provides private coaching to guide authors through the writing, publishing, and online marketing processes.

Kathy is a popular keynote and conference speaker, mentor, and writing consultant. In 2021 she began co-hosting the now widely popular podcast Writing Works Wonders with Cheryl. This podcast serves as inspiration, encouragement, and skill-building for writers of all skill levels. In the early days of podcasting (2004-2010), she co-hosted and solo-hosted several others. Included among these series was the then-popular, Podcasts for Teachers.

As a professor for 30+ years, she was a researcher, administrator, and university educator. While her prior publications have been nonfiction, she is currently launching into science fiction fantasy writing. Her academic expertise spans adult learning, technology innovations, transformative learning, and instructional technology development.

Her 2018 book, "Technology and Innovation in Adult Learning," garnered the Textbook Excellence Award from Textbook and Academic Authors. (This book is available in print and digital format at Amazon and BookShare.)

In 2019, Kathy began losing her vision. Within two years, she was diagnosed with NAION — untreatable damage to the optic nerve, which thrust her into a blurry world called visually impaired/legal blindness. During this time, Kathy had to make the difficult decision to retire from her professorship.

Kathy has returned to her beloved mountains in Knoxville, Tennessee, where she continues to enjoy writing, podcasting, website development, virtual volunteering, public speaking, and coaching authors to use assistive technology.

CHERYL MCNEIL FISHER

Cheryl McNeil Fisher is an author who, for over 25 years, has been a national motivational speaker, workshop leader, and podcaster. Cheryl inspires audiences and readers to discover the strength to face setbacks and reach their dreams.

Cheryl advocates for children and adults with a full spectrum of unique traits in her career and volunteer work.

She co-hosts the widely popular podcast Writing Works Wonders with Kathy. She initiated Writing Works Wonders as a Zoom call through the American Council of the Blind. In the spring of 2021, she invited Kathy to join her as co-host on Writing Works Wonders. Part of the success of the series is the complementary nature of their personalities and skills, along with the dynamic team they have created.

Her publications range from fiction to nonfiction. Her creative children's books nurture imagination, goodness, kindness, and thankfulness while introducing the lifestyles of differently-abled people. Audiences benefit from Cheryl's counseling background through her positive, supportive perspective.

She uses technology extensively in marketing her book and author brand.

Since childhood, Cheryl has experienced low vision but, with contact lenses, had 20/30 vision. Then, in her early thirties, she experienced a sudden change that left her legally blind. "When life turns upside down, we grab on and make it the ride of our life!" Cheryl lives in the Hudson Valley with her husband, retired guide dog, Sanka, and current guide Raven.

ABOUT WRITING WORKS WONDERS

Vernon C. Henley Award 2022

Writing Works Wonders podcast garnered the 2022 Vernon C. Henley Media Award from the American Council of the Blind's Board of Publication. This much coveted award recognizes the outstanding contribution of this media production to serve the community of writers and readers who are visually impaired,

· increase our visibility as persons with disabilities, and provide a professional, positive model of empowerment and capability for society at large.

Encouraging, inspiring, and accelerating success among authors, is what the Writing Works Wonders podcast is all about! Authors Cheryl McNeil Fisher and Dr. Kathy King co-host this skill-building podcast for authors. But it's more than a podcast! Writing Works Wonders includes a website, newsletter, optional weekly writing prompt events, and a growing network of writers who meet on the Zoom calls.

Cheryl and Kathy record the weekly podcast via Zoom, with a live audience, at 1 pm Eastern most Friday afternoons. After polishing the edits, the podcast is distributed throughout the digital universe, where you can access it on your favorite podcast platform.

The noteworthy and varied format includes author interviews, workshops, Open Mics, Round Robins, panel discussions, and resources! Designed for new and experienced writers and authors, this engaging podcast provides opportunities to learn valuable skills, participate in live events, guest interviews, and strategy sessions.

The robust website (www.WritingWorksWonders.com) offers author resources, complete show notes, episode archives, and bonus content. From writing to publishing and marketing, the Writing Works Wonders team wants to help accelerate your success and ensure you discover the Wonders of Writing!

To join the email list, visit this link (https://bit.ly/WWWZoom) and complete the brief form. You will receive an email once a week, including the upcoming event description. The Zoom call information, the weekly writing prompts, and a sneak preview of the forthcoming events.

Email list sign up https://bit.ly/WWWZoom

INTRODUCTION

Welcome to a Writing Works Wonders' Special Edition Book. Who better to teach you how to design and maintain your website? We do it with our eyes closed. If we can do it blind, then you can too. Follow the step-by-step instructions we provide in this book and enjoy developing new capabilities!

We have enjoyed developing and growing the Writing Works Wonders Website. Kathy and her consulting groups, Transformation Education and now Writing Works Wonders, have worked with individuals and organizations to design and build their sites. And now it is your turn…

Our goal is to incorporate features that make sites appealing, informative, and accessible for visually impaired users while succinctly clarifying the message that meets the needs of your audience.

This book was born from Cheryl and Kathy's two-part series developed for the Writing Works Wonders author and podcast community. (www.WritingWorksWonders.com).

In addition to this book, you will have access to audio recordings with a companion resource page that provides the links cited throughout the text.

Chapter 10 is a copy of what is on that web page at the time of this book's development. It is meant to be evergreen to provide you with the latest information about website development. In addition, we hope you will benefit from the book's companion audios and resource page.

Link to companion resource page
https://writingworkswonders.com/author-resources/website-creation-for-authors/

CHAPTER ONE OVERVIEW

After decades of experience with multiple website development platforms, including HTML, we have chosen WordPress to be our platform of choice. Thus, in this book, WordPress will be the platform we discuss. Nonetheless, many of the stages may be used with any website platform. However, the development chapter will discuss specific instructions for WordPress.

Why did we make this choice? There are many reasons, and these will become clear as you proceed through each chapter.

YOUR ONLINE IDENTITY

Your website is the center point of your public identity and publicity efforts. The website is where people visit to learn about you, your books, your upcoming speaking engagements, and more. It can be an efficient and powerful resource to seamlessly integrate your social media, marketing, publicity efforts, email list, blog, and/or newsletter.

We have divided the many steps involved in website development into seven significant steps. This division offers a bird's eye view or perspective from start to finish. The chapters in this book provide accurate detail for each step but in easy-to-follow language. We also offer action questions at the end of each chapter that you may choose to complete or not. They will be helpful when you are ready to build your website and begin to follow the chapters. You might read this short book once or twice before answering the questions.

We intend the Follow Up Questions to encourage and guide you. And even better, there are no wrong answers! You are creating your website; you have the freedom to make these choices. We see our role as a guide walking next to you through the process, providing coaching and direction.

Bonus Tips and Hints are sprinkled through the book. They offer essential information in short snippets. Often, they help you avoid errors we have made! So, stay alert for these gems.

Remember, this book helps you create a unique, and distinctly yours, website! In this project, you are Master of the Universe! (More on that concept soon!)

OVERVIEW OF STEPS:

1. Identify Your Message.
2. Design and Layout
3. Select Web Platform
4. Select Web Hosting
5. Choose URL and Purchase.
6. Build the Site in Stages.
7. Incorporate Feedback and Improve.

Follow Up Questions Chapter 1:

1. What is the general focus or nature of your website design?
2. Who will most likely visit your website?
3. What is your budget?
4. Do you have a specific due date for the site? (Three months from now, twelve months from now, or six months before you release your book, etc.)

CHAPTER TWO
STEPS 1 AND 2
Identify Your Message, Design and Layout

Steps One and Two are so intertwined that we present and discuss them together in this chapter. Step One is to Identify Your Message, and Step Two is to Design and Layout the site that you would like to develop.

These two points need to be pursued simultaneously because they are the foundation of a great website. Identifying a relevant, straightforward message and the general way it will be communicated fit hand in hand.

I always recommend that people conduct an informal survey of other author websites and research what they like and don't like about those websites. Amid this research, authors may also ask which author website focus fits their efforts best. I suggest making a short list of what you discover, and gradually you will find that you focus on preferences for a key message and certain design styles.

Brand

When it comes to commercial products we use in our lives and homes, we are very familiar with brands. Famous examples of brands include Kleenex, Apple, and Honda.

When you look at book covers of best-selling authors, the author’s name and book title often are in the same size font, or perhaps the author's name is even larger than the title of the book! Why do we see this in books by authors such as James Patterson, C. J. Box, and others? It's because their names have become prominent brands.

Similarly, but on a smaller scale, when we begin to create our web presence, we contribute to building our brand as authors.

You can highlight your identity as an author and "grow" your author brand at this juncture. We usually suggest this approach for most authors' websites - focus your website message on you as the author.

The author becomes the hub, and the spokes of the wheel/website are the books, sales, marketing, speaking engagements, background information, mailing list, and possibly a blog or newsletter.

Step back with me for a moment. Consider how you decide on the next book to read. If you're like most people, you will often search for a familiar author, a recommended author, or popular book title. By focusing on your website and building your author brand and name recognition, you are helping to increase the odds that your book will come to mind for readers.

ABOUT PAGE

Other than the home page, the About page is the most visited page on most web sites. When you consider that one of the primary purposes of an author's website is to build brand and identification among readers, that's not surprising.

On your About page, be sure to list, at a minimum, the following information regarding your specific talents and uniqueness as an author.

- Brief welcome message to visitors and readers.
- Author professional photo.
- Brief author biographical sketch.
    - Why did you begin writing?

    - When did you start writing professionally?
    - What are your interests/ passions?
- Selected writing awards and honors received.
- Literary societies to which you belong.
- Life or professional experiences that contribute to your genre or storylines.
- Any other unique qualities that distinguish you as an author!

BUILDING YOUR CREDIBILITY

In addition to your past accomplishments and achievements,

your web audience will want evidence of your credibility. The Media page, which can be an independent page or a sub-menu page of the About page, greatly contributes to your credibility.

Your Media page may include,

* Detailed author biographical account, including all awards and honors.

* Articles, columns, blogs, where you have been published.

* Guest interviews.

* Guest blog posts.

* Other mentions in the media.

Another vital strategy is to post original content and updates to your site regularly through a blog or distribute a brief newsletter to subscribers. The latter option becomes a streamlined and effective opportunity to engage with your readers/audience.

In concluding this section, authors have several choices about the message for their website. While this is an individual choice, examining the web will reveal that most authors develop a main author website. Furthermore, authors tend to use their name as the url, such as www.RhysBowen.com

From that site, people learn about the author and her books. They also discover more about the author's accomplishments and activities, such as her availability for speaking engagements, teaching, or other projects.

That said, authors may also create websites for individual books or successful book series. However, we find that the best practice is for authors to have their own named website, which focuses on them as a professional and building their author brand.

The rather simple approach of examining different author sites may take some time. Usually, it is not accomplished in one sitting. However, it allows you to answer both critical questions through a coordinated effort.

2. PLAN YOUR DESIGN

You need to decide whether you want your website to have a basic design, book-focused, image-heavy, news/ post focused, or other choice. The main focus of the site will help narrow down the layout.

Relax! Reviewing other author websites will provide a good sense of what you are drawn to and what you don't like. Also, discussing website preferences with friends, colleagues, authors and people who buy your books provides additional valuable insight.

Our community, those who have visual impairment, tends to prefer more straightforward designs. We certainly stay away from moving figures, flashing messages, heavy reliance on graphics to convey our message, and we make sure that we use "ALT tags" for any graphics which are included.

Your website platform allows you to fill in a description for each graphic you include. This is called an "ALT tag" or "ALT description." The name "ALT tag" comes from the original website hypertext markup language (HTML) code designated field or attribute for this information.

You don't need to know all that, you will just fill in the image's description at the ALT tag so that screen readers can recognize the graphics and related information. Spending 30 seconds to include the ALT tag description when you add a graphic makes images screen reader-friendly. However, one must remember to do it for every graphic added to the website.

RECOMMENDATION

We recommend the theme for use in WordPress be screen reader-friendly, so we may address important accessibility issues with both the theme and other features.

And regarding low vision users, those who might use magnification with or without a screen reader, in WordPress, there is a simple feature, a plugin, that you may easily include in your site. This feature enables your website visitors to quickly switch the contrast, greyscale, font size, and other visual aspects to meet their visual needs. Again, in WordPress, it just requires a few clicks, and it will be available for all visitors to optimize their viewing options!

When we address accessibility in this book, we include accessibility for you as the author and website developer, as well as for your visitors.

DESIGN – STARTING POINT

BASIC - WHAT IS IT?

A basic design could be as simple as a single landing page. That is a home page which represents you or your work. Another common basic site is only three or four pages.

Which ones? Well, consider the essentials you look for when you visit a site. Most likely these pages include:

* Home

* About

* Contact Us, and in this case,

* Books or Content.

In fact, any of these are a good place to begin. Each provides a solid foundation for many authors beginning a website.

Did you catch that reference? Beginning a website. Our point is that you can begin with a basic site and then expand as time, opportunity and your career provide!

LAYOUT

With your survey of websites, consider the layouts which appeal to you as well. For example, do you prefer a graphic or header at the top of the page, with a menu and then content? Or a different layout? At this point, consider what might be simple at first, and what you might have in mind for further development. There is no harm in dreaming for the future and exploring possibilities.

Do you like the benefit of seeing some of the same features on each page? If so, sidebars or side columns are often used for this purpose. Sidebars may be on the right, left, or both sides of the screen. These, along with header (top of the page) and footer (bottom of the page) content, can be included in your design.

PURPOSE

The user or audience perspective. Based on your experience as a reader and author, why would people be visiting your site? Answer this question and then plan to incorporate that information for them.

In addition, remember to include your website goals and purposes as well. What is the focus of your site? Again, return to your message. Be sure the information for your message is also front and center for your visitors to find it easily.

On the home page, there are many features and much virtual "real estate" which offer opportunities to guide your visitors swiftly to the information you want to communicate in addition to what they initially seek.

Follow Up Questions Chapter 2:

1. Research the Message – As you looked at other websites, what were examples of author website key messages?
2. Based on your work as an author, what area would be a better focus for your site, you as the author, your book titles, the story world or character(s) for which you are known, or another message?
3. Write a one or two-sentence first draft of your site message and focus. Show it to a few colleagues for feedback. Now refine it.

4. Determine whether you will begin with a basic design. If so, what will be included in the original draft of your site (for instance, which pages)?
5. If you want to include more elements in your site, what type of design would you like, and what would be the elements? (Options may include sidebars, footers, blog, newsletter, podcast, etc.)
6. Which layout design do you prefer to use to begin your site? Jot down ideas.
7. What accessibility issues do you notice on any sites? This list will help you design a more accessible site. (Extra credit - Start a list and keep adding to it while you read this book.)

CHAPTER THREE
STEP 3
Choose Your Platform

There are many options for website platforms we might use. However, a free platform has drawbacks. It is not likely the best solution for a professional author website.

Some people use free platforms such as Wix, Blogspot, free WordPress, GoDaddy, SquareSpace, or other proprietary sites. Be aware that you need to consider crucial pros and cons carefully before making this decision.

KEY WEB PLATFORM CONSIDERATIONS

The key web platform considerations discussed in this chapter include

- Accessibility
- Capabilities
- Flexibility
- Transferability
- Ease of Use
- Restrictions

ACCESSIBILITY

As we mentioned in the previous chapter, accessibility for both designer and user is key for our community.

Therefore, we include a later chapter that explores accessibility in depth. At this point, it is critical to evaluate the accessibility capacity and barriers of any web platform under consideration.

CAPABILITIES

What are the capabilities of the different web platforms? While you currently have a specific goal and purpose in mind for your site, no doubt over the coming years, new opportunities will support future capabilities that you might not yet need to use.

Such capabilities might include, but not be limited to plugins, widgets, add-ons, calendar features, statistical reports and analytics, backup features, importing social media feeds, and integrating your social media posting. These are just a few examples of capabilities that you will see listed in the difference between web platforms.

FLEXIBILITY

A good choice for a web platform is one that is flexible. For example, will you have the capability to change the layout, theme, export and import images, etc., with the platform that you are considering? Or will you be confined to a limited number of options when it comes to the configuration?

TRANSFERABILITY

Once people build a site, there may come a time when the owner wants to move it to another website host and/or web platform. Would you be able to transfer your site to a different platform? If the site is proprietary like Wix, SquareSpace, Blogspot, and many others, the answer is no. You are locked into the chosen platform. If you outgrow the platform in the future, it doesn't meet your needs, or it's no longer available, you must rebuild your site from scratch. These examples illustrate the importance of considering whether you can be transferred to another platform or host in the future.

EASE OF USE

In terms of ease-of-use, we refer to learning to use these platforms and install, design, minor and major updates to the site, as well as security updates or upgrades.

Let's break this down a bit. First, I firmly believe that authors should be able to design and update their own sites. For most authors, this means being able to learn it. Our primary interest in life is writing and we're good at it. We don't need to invest copious amounts of time learning web design or technical web interfaces. Therefore, it's essential that the web platform you select is easy to learn to use and easy to implement the updates you need going forward.

The second issue is that it used to be quite difficult to change the comprehensive look of your website. It took a great deal of coding and time to be able to do this. However, it's as simple as clicking buttons with platforms like WordPress, that include ease of use for major themes and updates.

Finally, because of devious spammers and hackers, and the advancement of technology innovation, web platforms continue to need upgrades and updates for the platforms themselves, aside from your content. This is a part of life for website owners. Examine this feature of your potential web platform. A good choice is to able to click a button to accept the upgrade and the system installs it for you. Unfortunately, some systems still exist which require several steps of backup, download, and upload for upgrades. Beware of these because they can be complicated and cumbersome.

RESTRICTIONS

Free platforms come with explicit and implicit restrictions. That means that they might not be available for commercial purposes or organizations. It also can mean that you might be agreeing to ads, promotions, logos, or other advertisements on your site. Such marketing could reach beyond the web platform itself to commercial products or causes you would not be interested in supporting. In most cases, you don't have an opportunity to choose what the free web site provider displays on your site for advertising purposes.

Running technology services is not free. We know they all require electricity and equipment; therefore, these companies have to have a way to pay their bills! If you receive the platform for free, they have to cover their expenses somehow. So, go into the situation with eyes open.

SUMMARY

Since 2005, these issues have led me to switch exclusively to WordPress hosted website development on a hosting server. Let me explain, this is not the free WordPress that many people talk about. The next chapter will explain about choosing hosting services. It is a two-part deal. First, you purchase hosting space and then click a button to install WordPress. It's one of the many features included in the hosting service that you purchase as a bundle.

I have used this host and WordPress installation approach for at least 100 different clients over this time. Why? Because it is the easiest, most reliable, and most flexible platform to teach them so they can maintain a great site themselves. As a web designer, I consistently worked myself out of a job!

The web was envisioned as a virtual space where users could create their own content. WordPress fulfills this promise. The fact that over sixty percent of the world's websites use

WordPress demonstrates the robust capacity and flexibility of this platform as well.

IMPORTANT NOTE FROM YOUR AUTHORS

We are not in any way compensated by WordPress. Please be assured we derive no benefit of any kind for recommending this platform.

Follow-Up Questions Chapter 3:

1. Is the website platform I'm considering using accessible for myself and my future visitors?

2. If I desire, can I easily transfer my content to another platform in the future?
3. Is it easy for me to design and update my content?
4. Is it easy for me to install security updates and upgrades?
5. Does the platform I'm considering have the features I'm interested in at this point? (Come back to this question again, as you learn more about web design in later chapters.)
6. Are there any restrictions regarding the use of this platform?
7. What is the reputation of this website platform? (Look at comparisons on external sites, don't just rely on information provided by the company or site.)

CHAPTER FOUR
STEP 4
Select Web Hosting

WHAT IS WEB HOSTING?

The website host is where your website “lives." It is actually a computer server, connected to the Internet 24/7. It allows people to be able to access your site whenever they input your web address (your URL).

To explain this term, host, we use the analogy of a parasite and host from the animal world. The website lives on the host: examples of website hosting companies include HostGator,

GoDaddy, and DreamHost, to name only a few.

In order to build the type of complete website that we discuss in this book, you purchase a plan from them that is able to install WordPress.

The host company provides several services to you for a fee. You want to evaluate each of these offered services in order to see how well a potential host will fit your needs.

THE HOST PROVIDES:

- Server space for your website platform and your files to be installed and updated.

- Efficient support for your website traffic.
- Technical support for you.
- An email address related to the URL you chose.
- And an online interface for you to interact with the server. (You will need to do this occasionally when installing WordPress, making backups, etc.)

Today, hosting servers are large collections of interlinked computers which are directly connected to the Internet. That connection needs to stay active and available 24 hours a day, seven days a week. So, it's vital that your hosting company keeps that connection active and rapid. We all have experienced frustration when servers are slow, or unavailable.

Great news! Big hosting companies make inevitable server interruptions or failures invisible! If for some reason, there's a major power outage in the city where your host's computer network is, then automatically, their servers transfer incoming traffic to their computer backups in another part of the world. These extra installations are called mirror servers. So there's a complete backup of your website that your hosting company stores for you in several places around the globe.

I've actually experienced several instances where this was crucial for my website. In different cases, a widespread outage, local disaster, or computer virus infected part of the country. However, the disruption was not apparent because the system automatically transferred my website traffic to a mirror computer server in another part of the world or country.

Web hosts will provide technical support to assist you with set-up and troubleshoot any problems that you may experience. Therefore, before you sign up with a host, do your homework. Be sure of the availability and quality of the technical support they promise to provide.

Follow-Up Questions Chapter 4:

Choosing a website hosting company. You don't necessarily need to answer every one of these questions. But it is helpful to

explore most of the answers before making a final decision. If possible, you should also make sure you have a fourteen to thirty day period when you can cancel your hosting service with a money-back guarantee.

1. Which website platforms does the hosting company provide?
2. What is the interface for interacting with the server? (cPanel, Plex, etc.?)
3. What does the data say about the active and available time this hosting service provides their websites? (How often do their clients find their websites are not available?)
4. Is there a limit on how much traffic your website can support?

5. What are the different hosting plans available and features in each?
6. What hours and type of technical support do they provide? Phone? Chat? Email?
7. What is the reputation of their technical support customer service?
8. Is automatic backup of your website included in the plan you're considering?
9. Is the URL included in the purchase of your website space/ plan? (Often this small fee may be included for the first year only.)

CHAPTER FIVE
Choose a URL and Purchase

Now we finally discuss selecting the website address and how to purchase your URL! URL stands for uniform resources locator and it provides direct access to your site. It is the specific web address where people's websites exist. It is referred to as your domain within your hosting platform.

URLs are tracked and maintained in the international DNS (Domain Name Server). The DNS registry ensures that your URL, your domain, is yours and cannot be duplicated.

When you purchase your URL, you have ownership as long as you pay the annual fee. Think of it as renting. If you stop payment, the URL will return to the DNS registry for someone else to purchase.

Choices

Our fifth step of website development is, "Selecting a URL/ website address."

Possibility List

As mentioned above, your first choice of a URL might not be available; therefore, it's wise to have a shortlist of possibilities before you set about purchasing one. First of all, consider whether you want to use your name, or some version of your name, as the website address, or your book or series title. We strongly recommend that authors use their name in order to provide the ability for your website to be the focal point of your author brand and for all your publications. Having multiple websites can be not only time-consuming to maintain, but also costly.

That said, one website can have several URLs. For example, you could designate the primary web address and then use other URLs to redirect or forward to the same site. When users input any of the addresses, they arrive at the primary domain. Meanwhile, you only maintain one website.

This information assures you that your selection at this point does not have to be your one and only choice. Nonetheless, as you choose one to get started, keep it simple. You can build upon your site with alternative URLs, once you are familiar and comfortable with creating and maintaining your site.

Discuss your choice with a few colleagues or friends. If you have a common name such as Kathy King, you might have to consider other strategies for creating a URL. Here are some examples based on my name:

* DrKathyKing.com
* KathyKingAuthor.com
* Drkpking.com (I use this one, because professionally I am known and addressed as Dr. King.)

* TransformationEd.com (My consulting group dating back to 1991.)

When it comes to our web address, we may also use capital letters to our advantage! Each of the examples above uses capital letters to begin each word. For example,

KathyKingAuthor.com, has a capital K for Kathy, K for King, and an A for author.

I use this technique when I write out the web address to highlight the different words. It's a way to help our readers recognize and remember the URL. However, the great news is that web addresses are NOT case-sensitive. This means that visitors don't need to input the capital letters in order to reach the site! So, whether they use the capital letters or not, they still will reach your site.

Again, visit some author websites and notice what they use as their URL. Consider these questions during your exploration.

* Is the URL easy to remember?
* Is it difficult to spell?
* Which possibilities come to mind for your website?

BONUS HINT

Refrain from including dashes, hyphens, or periods in your URL. They will be difficult for your readers to remember.

Finally, as you build and add content to your site, the search engines will recognize the site and include it in their listings. Within a few months, when someone searches your name, your site will be listed.

URL Sources

We may purchase a URL from any one of several different sources. Below is a list of just a few that I have found to be reliable companies. Please note that you do not have to purchase your web address from the same company you host your website. In fact, many in the technical world find it is better to have the URL registered with a separate company. But, of course, you are "Master of the Universe," so you are free to make your own choice.

As of this writing, in 2022, generally, the price of URLs will be discounted for the first year, but after that most of them will be about $17.99 per year.

There are scores of sites where you might purchase URLS, but to ensure your money is well spent on reliable service, select a major vendor. The following list includes major URL purchase sites.

Where to Purchase a URL

* DreamHost.com
* GoDaddy.com
* HostGator.com

PROCESS STEPS

To proceed you must decide on a couple of possibilities for your website address and from whom you will purchase it. The URL includes two steps: determining its availability and purchasing it.

1. Availability

Go to the URL purchasing site, follow the steps to search for URL or name availability. Next, type or dictate the URL that you want to check.

The system quickly searches the entire international databases, the DNS, and indicates whether it is available for purchase. If it is, you may proceed. If not, the system automatically generates some other options. For us as authors, these are not usually great options. Ignore them! Instead, return to the list you created and type another option in the main dialogue box to determine its availability.

Also consider whether you might use a different ending for your URL. Extensions such as .net or .info are becoming more familiar to users. Some major authors such as C. J. Box have resorted to using them because of availability (CJBOX.net). Nonetheless, out of habit your users will generally try .com to find your site first. So try to make it easy for them!

2. Purchase

Finally, to purchase the URL, you click the selected URL and add it to your online cart. Once you proceed to checkout or purchase, the system will ask for your name, address, standard billing and payment information.

However, notice the charges carefully before you proceed, and review each item. For instance,

- Are you committing to purchase for one year or multiple years?
- Are extra services added on to your invoice?

At this point, you will likely see the option to pay for “privacy.” If you do not have a separate email and phone number for your website project, you might consider this privacy option. Otherwise, your information is listed in the DNS database and I can tell you that you will receive large numbers of calls from web developers and digital marketing enterprises for several months. They cull these DNS registration lists for new purchases to market their services. The privacy service fee shields you from such persistent communications. If you purchase the privacy protection, people will still find you on the web. The protection will solely ensure your contact information will not be in the public DNS database.

Depending on the company you select, you might input ownership details about your URL at the time of purchase or later.

The system will ask who owns the URL. They are actually asking who owns the intellectual property of the URL. In most cases, the person for which the site is being developed, in this case the author, will own the URL.

You will also need to include an address, email address, and in most cases a telephone number. Do not despair, this information can be changed in the future, but it is better to get it right the first time.

Click submit, or process.

Congratulations on your success, Master of the Universe! You now own a URL and have your specific website domain.

This URL is your intellectual property. Awesome!

We are tossing you some virtual confetti. Catch!

Follow-Up Questions Chapter 5:

1. Review some author websites, and jot down examples of their URLs.
2. Create a preliminary list of possible URLs you might use for your site. Mull the list over, share it with friends and colleagues for feedback and revise your list.
3. Visit some of the different sites where you may purchase a URL.
4. Ask friends which URL companies they use and how

their experience has been. Decide which one you will use.

5.
6. Follow the steps listed in this chapter to determine your URL choices availability and purchase your first author URL.
7. Celebrate a job well done!

CHAPTER SIX
Foundation of Accessibilities

In this book, we have mentioned accessibility several times. It should be clear that given that the book is about website development, we are specifically referring to web accessibility. However, that can mean a variety of things. So let's spell it out. First, this book specifically addresses developing websites that people with visual impairments can access. Furthermore, we address a seldom discussed topic, how people with visual impairment, including blindness, can develop websites.

The Many Types of Vision Loss

People who have visual impairments neither have all the same vision experiences, challenges, nor needs. This section of the chapter provides a very brief overview of some types of visual challenges and how people with these needs still navigate the online world when it is accessibly designed.

What Do We See?

BLINDNESS - Perhaps the most familiar vision loss that the fully sighted world is familiar with is the condition in which the person has little or no light perception and vision. But have you ever wondered what that exactly means? It can be a very different experience for individuals based on their eye condition/s and it's progression.

They might see: Total blackness, be able to tell if it is light or dark and some may see shadows.

LEGALLY BLIND – Severe vision loss has a legal definition in the USA of corrected sight no better than 20/200. That means what most people see at 200 feet is what people who are legally blind see at 20 feet. (Iowa Department for the Blind, 2022. https://blind.iowa.gov/legal-definition-blindness).

LOW VISION – While there are different definitions for this category, we will use the one widely used by the

American Optometric Association (AOA, www.AOA.org) and The Council of Citizens with Low Vision International (CCLVI.)

https://www.aoa.org/healthy-eyes/caring-for-your-eyes/low-vision-and-vision-rehab?sso=y

People have low vision when, even with lenses, their sight cannot be corrected beyond 20/70-20/200)

* There is a tremendous variety of vision differences in this range, and there are numerous causes for the vision loss. Here are a very few of the many characteristics some people experience, plus they may have multiple traits mixed together. Most of all, there are many variations for each trait we describe. There are likely no two people who are exactly the same.

SELECTED LIST OF VISION TRAITS

* Central vision, no peripheral vision, which doesn't mean simply tunnel vision.
* More peripheral than central vision.
* Blotchy and/or blurry vision.
* Multiple blind spots.
* Color blindness – entire or partial.
* Fully Sighted/Correctable Vision – These are the folks who can see close to 20/20 -20/60 with or without glasses, contact lenses, or surgery. They have correctable vision. In the community of visual impairment, we refer to people with this visual acuity as "sighted."

Reading these descriptions should bring some observations to mind. It may be difficult to figure out which category fits an individual's experience.

In addition, people may switch categories across their lives. Our sight might get better or worse.

Even if we are fully sighted for most of our life, we might shift to another category at some time.

All three points are absolutely true. We never want to rigidly assign someone to a category as their permanent condition! Neither do we ever want to make someone's identity equal to their condition or their diagnosis. Instead, these terms are ways to help us talk about our experiences with others to gain support, educate and learn.

Timing of Sight Loss

In addition to complete or partial vision loss, another important dimension is time. If someone has never been fully or partially sighted or has no memory of vision (maybe they became blind before the age of 2), their understanding of the "visual world" will be very different from someone who lost their sight as a teen, adult, or even recently.

This concept is not easy to unpack. However, we want to introduce the concept that some individuals with visual impairment have had fully or partially sighted life experience.

Another point to consider is that people without any vision currently have mental constructions based on various sources. These might include visual experiences if they previously had sight, written descriptions, sensory experiences, or other input.

WHAT ABOUT WEB ACCESSIBILITY?

Moving back to our website design discussion, you can see that we have a wide variety of vision issues to address in web design. Why? Because the great news is that people with visual impairment, no matter how severe, have ways to navigate the Internet when websites are designed accessibly.

Readers might wonder how do people with limited or no vision access the web if they cannot see the websites? Today's technology has come a long way, and we hope tomorrow's will be even better! Here are a few of the ways website visitors who are visually impaired will try to access and navigate your site. And we will help you be ready to successfully address their needs.

TECHNOLOGY USED

SCREEN READERS - This is specialized text to speech (TTS) software used to read text on a screen aloud to the user. Using Heading styles in your website text and ALT tags for your graphics will be strategies you need to consistently incorporate for screen readers to work well. We will discuss these shortly.

Screen reading programs include JAWS, NVDA, and those built into computer operating systems like Windows Narrator®, and iOS VoiceOver.

MAGNIFICATION – Website users may use separate programs to magnify all or part of the screen.

Magnification programs include Zoom Text ®, or those built into the operating systems such as Windows Magnify®, or iOS Zoom.

WHAT DOES ACCESSIBILITY MEAN FOR THE WEBSITE VISITOR?

It's really pretty easy when you think about it. Web accessibility means that people using any of these technologies, or a combination of them, (screen readers, magnification, etc.) should be able to interact with your site successfully. They should be able to:

* Find the information they want.
* Complete online forms.
* Listen to multimedia.
* Purchase items such as your books, if they are for sale.
* Participate in dialogue.
* Contact you.
* Engage in and enjoy everything available to your sighted visitors.

Other than common sense, courtesy, and good business, why is accessibility important? Because it is the right thing to do and it is the law. Building upon the 1990 Americans with Disabilities Act (https://www.ada.gov/ada_intro.htm), in 2010, the revisions to Titles II and III of the ADA were passed. These included websites for the first time in the updated ADA Accessibility Standards (https://www.ada.gov/2010ADAstandards_index.htm). Thankfully, as technology changes, these requirements continue to be updated to keep pace.

To make things very clear for website developers, there are even web accessibility guidelines. These lists are rather technical, but here they are. Do not be overly concerned. We include the essential items you need to know and follow in this short book.

SPECIAL NOTE

We provide direct links to these standards because we strongly suggest that in this case, you do NOT use your search engine. Such searches will usually lead to many commercial products, which are costly and may not always completely work. These links are for your reference. We will make website accessibility easy for you because of the web platform, WordPress, and plugins we recommend. However, we want you to be able to access the source material.

WEB ACCESSIBILITY LINKS

WCAG – Web Content Accessibility Guidelines – Recommendations to support compliance with ADA requirements for web accessibility

- Complete information for individuals planning and designing websites. W3.org
- Create an Accessibility Policy – Use this free tool to generate an Accessibility Policy/Statement for your website. https://www.w3.org/WAI/planning/statements/generator/#create
- Web Accessibility Checklist from ADA.gov https://www.ada.gov/pcatoolkit/chap5chklist.htm

SUMMARY

We have explored the practical concept of and need for web accessibility. This chapter also briefly discussed different types and experiences of vision loss. Finally, we introduced the legal guidelines for web accessibility and that we will incorporate these needs in website design. Onwards and upwards!

Follow-Up Questions Chapter 6:

1. What did you learn about the types and experiences of vision loss?
2. If you are not familiar with screen readers or screen magnification, conduct a web search and read more about how people use them. It's really helpful to understand how users might interact with your site.
3. Have you ever visited a website and been frustrated because the

checkout system did not work well or you received error messages when you tried to access information? Jot down some of your feelings at that time.

4. Guess what? Those experiences you had are much like what an inaccessible website experience can be for individuals who are visually impaired!
5. In the past, what has encouraged you to send a complaint or suggestion to a website owner or webmaster?
6. How will you encourage visitors to let you know if they are having difficulties with your site?
7. On your site, what contact information will you be comfortable providing for this purpose?

CHAPTER SEVEN STEP 6: Build the Site in Stages

Keep Your Visitors on Your Site!

As authors, we are well aware of the need to capture the attention of our readers and maintain their attention. We need to understand our audience and what they expect from our work. Whether it is mystery romance, science fiction, poetry, blog entry, the great American novel, journalistic report, nonfiction, or fiction, the principle is the same.

However, with your website, you have 10 to 30 seconds, that's it! When it comes to keeping your readers on your website to learn about you and your work, you only have about 10-30 seconds to capture their interest.

These figures are based on the most current research of website user habits. Clearly, we must capture site visitors' attention before they leave. And that same research demonstrates that it's not all about color and splashy images because people are searching for content and do not want to wait for images or videos to load. Moreover, among visually impaired users, from color blindness to low vision and blindness, they might not even see colors and images.

This limited time frame is even more challenging than what a reader allows for in our extended prose or poetry writing.

What are the crucial elements we need to display and communicate in this short window of opportunity? It's the message and navigation. Most users subconsciously assess sites based on two characteristics.

- How prominent, clear, concise, and quickly do you communicate your message to your site visitor?
- How easily can users navigate your site to find what they want?

While it's great to be innovative with what you offer on your site and in your writing, you don't want to confuse people with your website. We all can recall examples of sites that were too confusing, and we just bailed and went on to the next site in frustration.

Maybe you couldn't find

- The cart to checkout for your purchase.
- The descriptions of the products you were considering buying.
- The return policy.
- The contact information.
- You fill in the blank!

We know the difficulties. We don't want to mirror those issues for our users.

So, as you launch into building your site keep your message and navigation in mind. 10-30 seconds that’s it my friends! Hook their interest quickly.

BUILDING BASICS

The fundamental approach to building your website is to work in stages.

* Build the skeletal structure; the barebones of your website.
* Add the major functions.
  * Begin to fill in -
    * Your biographical information.
    * Welcome or Home page information.
    * Book synopsis and imagery (such as book covers, your professional photo, etc.)
    * Contact page.
    * Additional images
      * Next, you might add important, selected images which complement the content on your site.

PRIORITIZE YOUR DESIGN WORK

Consider and address the basics first. I like to get those in place the way we want them and then fill in more details within and around the basic structure.

Overall, you want to keep clean lines, or view, of your site, not cluttered. This principle is important for visitors who are sighted and visually impaired alike. This practice means we incorporate universal design principles, which results in our design being accessible to all individuals.

STARTING WELL

Begin inputting your site's most critical information first, then gradually add further detail.

Result: You will be sure to have the most critical information in place.

If the site begins to look (or sound in the case of a screen reader or VoiceOver) cluttered, of course, you modify it. Options for reshaping your page and site may include, moving content to other pages, submenus, sidebars, footers, headers, and more.

Bonus TIP

If you have too much content, never just delete it! Instead, I highly suggest you copy and paste it into a word processor or text editing program for safekeeping. That way, you will not have to recreate it! You will just copy and paste it when you are later ready to use it.

BRINGING IT ALL TOGETHER

Short Activity Interlude!

You now have an idea of where we are headed with this chapter on building the site. Before we move into more technical steps, let's reflect on the concept of navigation and design.

You might ask, what are some simple examples of website design conventions users expect? What do they expect when it comes to navigating sites?

Guess what? You know the answers to these questions. I know you do!

Think about when you are on a website, "What side of the screen or a menu do you expect to find "About Us?"

(Pause and think of the answer…)

You knew it! It's usually at the beginning of the menu, over to the left.

And answer this one, "What side of the screen or a menu do you expect to find "Contact Us?"

(Pause and think of the answer…)

Awesome! Contact Us is over near the end of the menu, usually to the right.

And the Cart button?

Right again, it will be near the Contact Us menu item.

These are examples of predictable locations for features on most sites, which can be beneficial. Why? Because we all know frustrated visitors leave websites. And for some reason, many people hesitate to access the Search or Help features.

So do some exploring, discuss your plans with friends, and ask them what do they expect for website navigation? Take notes!

Next, talk to people that buy your books and ask them what are the most important things they want to be able to find quickly.

We are sure you can anticipate this suggestion, visit some of those great author websites you like, and see how they are set up! Compile a list so you will have suggestions for planning and designing a site that has those features readily visible.

Instructions for WordPress

These are instructions for installing WordPress, on a hosting service, and then beginning to build your site.

(If you use the free WordPress site, without a paid hosting plan, these will not be the exact steps.)

We begin with an overview of the steps to set up your skeletal structure. You will have your basic site constructed by the end of these steps!!

We promise this is not difficult. We will walk through each step.

WordPress Setup Overview

1. Install WordPress
2. Login to WordPress
3. Fill in Site Identity
4. Install a Theme
5. Create Pages
6. Create a Menu

7. Setup Your Homepage
8. Install Plugins
9. Add Widgets
10. Assess and Revise
11. Fill-in Content

So as we say on Writing Works Wonders, put on your party hat. It's time to have fun and start building your website!

Walking Through WordPress Setup

1. Install WordPress

This installation is usually a one-click function. Once you purchase your hosting plan, you receive login information.

Login to the server platform, it may be called CPANEL, or PLEX for instance. Now find the area that is labeled "install website packages" or a similar title.

You should find an option for WordPress. Click it and fill out the fields with the name of the URL you purchased, the name you are thinking of for your site, your main email address, and create a strong password, and anything else it might ask. Finally, click the submit button, and it should install WordPress in about 3-10 minutes.

2. Login to WordPress

You will receive an email with the details of how-to login into your

WordPress account,

Yes, this is entirely separate from your server account. Click the link, save it to your desktop for later use and use your email and the password you chose to login.

Voila, you have installed WordPress and logged into the administrative control panel. In WordPress, this area is called the Dashboard.

3. SET YOUR THEME

While there are thousands of themes available to select among, we highly recommend the WordPress theme GeneratePress. This particular theme is compatible with screen reading programs for both the web development and user sides. This recommendation is based on Kathy's research that GeneratePress is the most widely used in our community of people who have visual impairments and her own experience with it. While many WordPress themes can be made accessible for visitors using screen readers, this one is unique in its purposeful accessibility for the developers.

That said, you are welcome to explore and experiment with themes that have different features to determine if they work well for you. As I, Kathy, have lost more sight and am helping more people who are blind, GeneratePress has become my go-to theme.

Also, do not worry; most themes, including GeneratePress, may be customized to a great degree. There are countless options and variables to select to tailor your site to your needs and design dreams, making your site look different from other designers'.

Log into WordPress; you should be at the Dashboard. If not, go to the upper left corner and click Dashboard.

Now go to the Main Menu on the left-hand side, click Appearance, and then select Themes.

This is where you may review different installed themes or search for and install new ones. Most themes are at least free to try.

Remember, the theme is not your content but the overall layout and still includes many options. The point is you are not changing your site content when you select or test a new theme.

In the future, when you have content posted. You can try a new theme and your site's words and images all remain the same.

After you select a theme, such as GeneratePress, now click Install. Then click Activate. Finished! Great work!

Theme Set-up Summary

Go to the Dashboard

Click Appearance

—— Themes

——— Select a Theme

———— Click Install

————— Click Activate

4. Site Identity (Appearance)

Again, in the WordPress dashboard, go to the Main Menu on the left side and click Appearance,

Customize, the Site Identity and input the name and subtitle of your site, which may show up in the layout of your website's header.

In this section, also make an initial decision about your design layout. Options include having one, two, or no sidebars or columns, on your site. The sidebar (a narrow column) could be on the left, center, or right side of the screen.

As you explore the options in this section, under Typography you will be able to adjust the font style and size for the whole site.

Much like in a word processor, websites now use heading styles: Paragraph P, Heading 1, H1, Heading 2, H2, Heading 3, H3, etc. This Typography section provides global access to the settings for each of these styles.

What does this mean? If you change your paragraph style to Arial 18, then all your basic content on the site will be in that font type and size. When you change H1, to Arial 36, bold then any text you designate as Heading 1 text will have that font size and type.

However you work in the customize theme screen, be certain to click Publish (at the top of the column you are working in) to save your changes.

If you don't, you guessed it, Poof! They disappear and you have to make them again.

Now, this part is really exciting for web designers. Are you ready?

Later, if you decide to change H1 from 36 to 43 or any other font size or type, you just change it here, and immediately, every occurrence of H1 text in your entire site is updated. You do not have to visit each page and change the font size or type.

I told you it was awesome! Now, who is Master of the Universe? You are!

For ease of reading and accessibility, we recommend a non-serif font, like Arial. Non-serif means the font type does not have extra tails or curls on the ends of the letters. It is much easier for individuals with limited vision to distinguish among and read san serif characters.

Site/Font Setup Summary

Appearance

— Customize

—— Site Identity

——— Make Changes

———— Click Publish

Appearance

— Customize

—— Typography

——— Make Changes

———— Click Publish

BONUS TIP

As Master of the Universe, you are free to determine what works best in the font styles and sizes. So, try them out and change them based on your own and your visitors' needs. However, keep an eye on the web accessibility standards, it recommends San Serif and a larger font size.

5. Create Pages

Wow! **You are making great progress!** We will now begin creating web pages. I suggest you begin with four to five main pages that all your visitors will likely expect to find, and we will incorporate the accessibility guidelines as we progress.

Preliminary Web Pages

These are just rough drafts of your pages to get you started. Don't be concerned about fine-tuning your content details yet.

1. About- Include your name and what type of work you write.

2. Home - Draft a sentence of greeting to your web visitors.

3. Detailed Content Page – Will you highlight one book, a series, or

your upcoming book? List it here and enter a description. For your book description, you might just start with the description on the back cover.

4. Contact Us – Enter a sentence that says, please contact us with any questions. Do not put in your email address yet.

5. Accessibility Policy- We will provide information about following the guidelines and how users may let you know if they encounter accessibility issues.

At this point, you only need to insert a few words on each page. They will be placeholders, and you will return later and work on them.

For each page, you will follow the same process.

a) Go to the Dashboard, click PAGES in the left-hand main menu. (Make sure you select PAGES and not POSTS.)

b) Then click ADD NEW.

c) When the next screen appears, In the box labeled ADD TITLE, fill in the title of the page (such as About, Home, Contact Us, My Books, etc.).

d) Press the tab key, and your cursor will be in the large box/field, which is your page content box. This is laid out much like a word processor with options for bold, italic, etc.

e) For now, in this area, simply fill in a few words or one sentence relevant to that page.

f) Once completed, go to the right-hand side of the screen and look, or listen, for the word Publish.

Click that, and your page is live on the web!

g) You may Preview your page to see what it looks like to visitors by clicking the Preview button up near the Publish button.

h) Once you are finished looking at it, click the browser's Back button to return to the WordPress dashboard and the page you created.

Whoop! Whoop! The first page is completed! Let’s move on to the next.

Move to the top of the page, click Add New. A new blank page appears, and you follow the same steps you did before. Start creating the next page on your list!

PAGES

— ADD NEW Page

—— Add Content

——— Click Publish

When you have completed the pages, you need to celebrate your progress again!

You have made major strides in building your site. You are well on your way.

We will shortly show you how to edit these pages. Let's continue learning to add additional, important website features.

6. Create Menu

Remember how important we said navigation was for a website? The menu is a crucial part of that. In this section, you will create your navigation menu and discover how easy it is to rearrange the menu choices in the future. Across the life of your site, you will receive feedback and add and move pages as your site matures. That is why you will rearrange your menu and WordPress makes it really easy.

In the Dashboard, click Appearance and then click Menu, which will be near the middle of the list. This action opens a different type of screen.

Near the top will be two tabs. One is to edit the menus, and the other is menu locations. We will work on the main menu first.

So, click Menu location and select where you would like it to be displayed on your site. There are several self-explanatory options listed.

Now click the Edit Menu tab. Be sure the menu title is main menu, if it is not, flip open this box and select it.

On the left of the Edit Menu page, there will be a list of all the pages you have created. On the right is a list of the items in your selected menu.

Whenever you create new pages, you should come back to this menu option and add the page to the menu.

1. Review your menu list (on the right), are any items in there?
2. If all the pages are in the menu list, skip the next step.
3. If any or all of the pages are missing from the menu list, go to the list of created pages.

a. Select each page you need to add to the menu.

b. At the bottom of the box/field, click on Add to Menu.

c. Now return your focus to the menu list on the right.

ALERT If your pages do not appear in the left-hand list, go back to the

Pages option in the Dashboard, click All Pages and see if it says DRAFT next to the page name. If any do, you must open each and Publish them. Alternatively, you might have created posts instead of pages by mistake. Go back and rebuild them as Pages.

4. You may re-order the items in the right-hand side Menu list (the four or five pages) by dragging them with your mouse. Another way to move them is to click each open, and you should see options to Move Up or Move Down the entry in the list!
5. A Submenu can be created by clicking "Move." However submenus involve a workaround for accessibility. Rather than interrupt our discussion here, we explain the steps to create screen

reader/JAWS accessible submenus in Appendix C.

a. Here are the basic steps for making a submenu. For instance, you might move the Accessibility Policy page to just below the Contact Us page in the list.

b. In the menu list, click the tab or Open Accessibility Policy options,

c. Click "Move Under Contact Us."

d. And you will notice it is now indented.

e. Click OK in that same box.

6. But you are not finished yet. Save, Save, Save! You must save your work when you are in the Menu system, or all your work will vanish! The save feature is in the bottom right-hand corner of the menu box. So do not forget to click

the save button, or you will need to repeat your work. (We know this error all too well!)

Menu Set-up Summary

Appearance

— Menu

—— Menu Location

——— Edit Menu

——— Click Save

VIRTUAL FIELD TRIP!

LET'S SEE MENUS IN ACTION! GO VISIT www.CCLVI.org and examine the menu just below the header that has the title of the website.

What are the main items in the menus?

What are the submenu items in each? Some of the Main Menu items do not have submenus, can you determine which ones?

Of course, it is not the perfect website! So, we provide this example for you to see what we are learning in practice.

Navigation Menus v. Content

You will also notice, for example, if you visit our site www.WritingWorksWonders.com once a week, our content will change. However, since we built this in 2021, at this point, our menus, like those at CCLVI.org don't change too frequently.

7. Set Your Homepage

When you visit a website, the first page you land on is called the home page. You have the opportunity to select your homepage now.

Usually, you will select your About page or Welcome page as the home page. This is very easy and never has to be done again unless you decide to change your selection.

Summary

Set Your Homepage

Go to the Dashboard

— Settings

—— Reading

—— In the section labeled, "Your homepage displays"

———— Of the two radio buttons, click "A static page"

————— Homepage, select the page you want from the combination box

———— Click Save Changes

8. Install Plug-ins

One of the features we appreciate the most about WordPress is the vast number of add-on features available through easy-to-use plug-ins and widgets. Not only are they available right within the WordPress dashboard, but most require only one click to install!

Plug-ins are small programs that developers create to run as add-ons to WordPress for very specific purposes. In some ways, plug-ins are much like smartphone apps. At the same time, just like smartphone apps, there are usually several Plug-ins from which you may choose for some functions, and you can find user reviews and ratings of them.

Unlike your smartphone, you do not have to go to a separate application to retrieve plug-ins (the Appstore or Google Play). Instead, you may access them through the Wordpress dashboard. Here are the steps and a partial list of some of our favorite WordPress plug-ins along with their functions. A complete list will be found in the final chapter, along with the companion web page!

The following list provides some basic, free plug-ins which provide accessibility features, an interactive calendar, statistics, email lists, broken link checker, WordPress backup, security, and many advanced and automated functions.

Recommended Plug-ins

Accessibility

- One-Click Accessibility
- Accessibility Tool and Alt Text Finder

Backup

- UpDraftPlus Backup/Restore

Broken Link Checker

- Link Checker

Button Maker (Accessible buttons)

- MaxButtons Form Maker

- Ninja Forms
- WPForms
- MailerLite Form plugin for MailerLite email list system
- MailChimp plugin for MailChimp system

Payment Processing

- WP Easy PayPal Payment Accept
- WP PayPal

Podcasting

- Pinecast WordPress Sync
- WP RSS Aggregator

Security

- WordFence Security

Social Media

- Social Media Follow Buttons Bar

Statistics

- Rank Math SEO
- WPStats

From the list, we will use the One-Click Accessibility plugin as an example to demonstrate how to install plug-ins. We selected One-Click Accessibility because it is free and provides a simple, but effective way to enable visually impaired users to customize their view of your screen for them to be able to navigate it more easily. (We are incorporating following the 2010 Web Accessibility Guidelines!)

Follow the steps below to install One-Click Accessibility. Then, later, come back and explore some other plug-ins in the list and determine if you want to install and configure them. We hope you will enjoy discovering how they work tirelessly for you and your site!

Plug-in Instructions

Go to the Dashboard,

Click Plugins

Click All Plugins- Now, you may review which ones are already installed.

Click Add Plug-ins – This option is available at the top of your screen. Whenever you want to add a new Plug-in to your list.

Go to the search box on this screen and paste or type in One Click Accessibility.

When you see it in the list, click on the Install button.

Next, click the Activate button for that plug-in.

Plug-in Hint: All plug-ins will either display instructions on the screen, on the plug-in page, or a new menu item might be added to your Dashboard. Open the information file or visit the plug-in web page when all else fails.

These are the configuration steps that specifically apply to One-Click Accessibility.

One-Click Accessibility Setup

Once the plug-in is installed and activated (above), proceed.

Go to the Dashboard

If you have GeneratePress installed,

- Scroll down, to Appearance, then click Customize, scroll down to and click Accessibility.
- You will find several options available. Explore these to select where you want the accessibility icon to appear on your site (right or left side) and whether you wish to use the other default settings or change some of them.
- Then, be sure to click Publish at the top right of the column.
- Save, Save, Publish, Publish....

You are a real website developer now!

Step 8 Plugins Setup Summary

Plugins

— All Plugins

— Click Add Plugin

—— Click Install

——— Click Activate

————- If required, configure the plug-in

9. Add Widgets

Widgets are different from plug-ins in that they usually do not add extra features; instead, they provide streamlined ways to display your content in different areas of your site. For example, you can use widgets to insert images, social media posts, your books, menus, and more in your website sidebars, headers, and/or footers.

Process to Install WordPress Widgets.

Go to the Dashboard

Click Appearances

Click **Widgets**

Click Footer 1 (Footer 1 is one widget region example.)

Let's select the region of the site in which you want to add a widget. Let's start with the footer as an example.

In this field, click the PLUS sign and select Text from the list of options. If it is not readily evident, start typing in the word "text" in the search bar, and it should appear.

This provides a text field for you to complete. Type the following in the box to include a copyright statement for your website

Copyright, 2022, your name.

Then on the right-hand side of the screen, click Save or Publish. Guess what happens if you forget to do that? Yes, it's gone.

If you selected sidebars for your site, you may also select the left or right sidebar and include a widget there. Visit some sites and notice what authors include in sidebars. Here are some sidebar widget possibilities.

- Image widget – To include a photo of your recent book, which should also link to the web page about it.
- Social media - Links to your social media pages.
- Link or an image for a special offer available on your website.
- Link to your Contact Us page or eMail List Sign-up page.

Just start with one or two widgets for now. After that, you can add, delete, and edit them into eternity! At this point, we wanted you to know how easy this feature is and begin to understand some of the widget capabilities.

Widgets Setup Summary

Dashboard

—Appearance

— Widgets

—— Select a region

——— Add widget type

———— Add content

————— Click Publish

10. ASSESS, AND REVISE

You have completed the bare bones of your website; this is your skeletal structure. Now is the time to sit back and ask a few questions.

- What do I need to update and add next, first, second and third?
- How much time can I allocate to this project weekly to gradually fill it in enough to reveal it to the world?
- Do I have a date or event for which I need this ready?

These are helpful points to ponder now and into the future. They will help you set goals and realize you do not need to have a huge site built in a week. Instead, start out small, explore and enjoy the creativity.

Additional suggestions for developing your site further include,

- What additional pages should I include?
- Will a blog be of interest to my visitors?
- And do I have time to do this occasionally?
- Will a mailing list be helpful?
- Should I revise the titles of the pages?
- Does the menu need rearranging?
- Which widgets and plugins will help me serve my visitors well now, and which can be added later?
- Which plug-ins will increase the functions and efficiency of my site? (We suggest installing

Backup and Stats plugins as soon as possible.)

You will gain feedback, contemplate and revise this site more times than it seems you breathe! You are not paying anyone to do all these updates! That is another benefit of maintaining your own site.

Consider your goals for your site and what your intended/target audience will look for on your site.

- How will you make it easy to find and navigate?
- How will you keep it attractive and accessible?

11. Add Content

Now is the time to return to your skeletal site and begin to fill in the content. Review the pages you have created and begin gathering or composing content for the pages.

Adding Images

First, we will add an image to one of your pages. Identify where you have saved an image of yourself or one of your book covers on your computer. Specifically, what folder it's in. Just for practice, we will add it to your About page. You can always delete it; not to worry.

Although, the instructions look a little longer on the page. You will have this process mastered after you have uploaded one or two photos. It is very easy to follow along on the screens. We provide the details so that you do not have to guess what to do next.

Go to the WordPress dashboard. Next click pages, then All Pages. Select the About page from the list that is in front of you. Click Classic Edit.

Next, move your cursor to below the words you have on this page.

Now go up and click Add Media. This means that you may add images, documents, audio, or video. It will take you to your Media Library within WordPress.

Click Add New or Upload. Now select the file you have in mind in your computer folder. And click Select or

Open. It will upload it to the server and connect it to WordPress.

When the image comes up on the screen, click it and move to the field which is labeled “ALT description”, this is the ALT tag we mentioned earlier. In this field, enter "Photo of the author, my name."

You may also add a description of the image. Such as “Photo of the author, Kathy King. Woman with silver hair, and blue eyes who is smiling and wearing an orange suit jacket.”

Notice that in the lower right-hand corner, there is the option to insert the image to the left, right, or middle of the line. You flip open a box to select among these options. You can also change the size of the image so that it's the actual size, large, medium, custom, or thumbnail, which is 150 x 150 pixels. Pick thumbnail for now. Then click Submit, which is at the very bottom right corner of this screen.

Your image will be on the page. Click Update or Publish to save the image on the page.

Summary - Add an Image to a Page

Go to the Dashboard

— Pages

— All Pages

—— Click the page you desire to edit

—— Move the cursor below the text on the page, click Add Media

—— Click Upload or Add New

—— Select your image, and upload it

——— Click on the image and fill in Alt Description.

________ Review location & image size

__________ Click Submit

____________ Click Update or Publish

Another major accomplishment!
Hurrah!

Updating Content

We highly recommend drafting your website text in a full word processing program (i.e., Word, Pages, GoogleDocs, etc.) so you may diligently use the full features of grammar- and spell-check. Once you have edited and refined your content, then copy and paste it into your website pages.

Once you paste in the text, you should go through and add the heading formatting for the major sections of your page. Your title should be in style H1 and your next level headings H2. The text of the paragraphs should be in paragraph formatting.

You know by now the mantra of save, save, save whenever you make changes!

Your main pages will be created and edited under the Pages option in the WordPress dashboard. However, when you want to edit blog posts (which we discuss shortly), those will be in the Post feature.

HINT - Pages and Posts- What's the difference?

At first, some people are confused between pages and posts in WordPress. The difference is really quite easy. Pages are your more static web page content. Whereas Posts are your individual listings of information that are time-sensitive and more often identified by the date they were published on the web. The older items are listed below, the newer posts.

For functional purposes, the posts belong to the blogging feature of WordPress, whereas the Pages relate to the website structure.

Examples

Author #1's website might have all the standard menu items, but also an Update or Latest News area. When you click on these sections, you find content listed according to the posting date.

The newest posts are at the top of the list. They are usually categorized or have tags associated with the post, making it easier for visitors to find information they are interested in, such as public speaking, travel, etc.

In fact, this "News" section is most likely a blog, while the other items in the menu are the site's web pages.

Author #2's website might have a menu which includes a page titled Podcasts, taking them to a separate page highlighting the monthly podcast episodes.

Each episode has a number, title and short description to entice the visitor to:

1. Click here to play episode now.
2. Click here for more information.
3. Click on your favorite podcast app (the icons are shown on page) and subscribe to be notified of the latest episodes.

Author #2 used the same structure as Author #1, except that instead of a written blog, we could say she has an audio blog. The podcast episodes are integrated into the website with a podcast plug-in that creates a new post for each episode.

TRIVIA BONUS - In the early days of podcasting, circa 2004, we referred to podcasts as audio blogs because most were posted through blogs.

There are many ways to display your content, many options for using posts and pages, and an infinite number of possibilities as to what to include in your site's overall content.

Again, this is your site, so you are Master of the Universe and can make the choices that you believe will best meet your needs. If they don't work as well as you like, you change them! What terrific opportunities and freedom you have in this project.

Add Content Summary

Updating Pages

—-All Pages

—--Select Page to Edit

—— Edit Classic

——— Click Update

Updating Posts

— All Posts

—-Select Post to Edit

—— Edit Classic

——— Click Update

Follow-Up Questions Chapter 7:

1. Consider a timeline for completing your website's development. You might want

to complete only two or three steps a day.

2. Continue to review different websites and examine the different features discussed in his chapter. Make brief notes, so you know which ones you want to consider for your own.
3. Review the content on different authors' websites and consider what content you already have on your computer. I greatly believe in repurposing content. If you already have a terrific 200-word biography, use it on your site.
4. Draft a welcome page and let friends review it. Consider their input, make final choices, and add it to your site.

5. Identify which materials you already have to describe your work and revise them to match the venue of a website.

6. Start listing, and later, drafting new materials you need for the site.

Chapter EIGHT

STEP 7: Incorporate Feedback and Improve

Stage Seven is one of ongoing, continuous improvement. This is why it's so very important on many levels that we are able to maintain our websites ourselves. It is the fundamental reason why Kathy switched to WordPress, using a separate hosting service back in 2005. WordPress enables Kathy's consulting group to design a website, then transfer maintenance and revision responsibility to the individuals and companies who have hired her. WordPress is a non-technical platform on which most people can build and maintain their own sites.

Website Rule of Success –

A powerful website is one that is kept updated. A static, out of date, website is useless.

We have described a few ways that we can feed continuous new information into our websites. But we also need to have a process to easily receive feedback from site visitors. We need to know what they're looking for, what they need, and if they are encountering any difficulties accessing information.

Most of the comments authors receive on their websites are about their work. It's terrific to know that our readers enjoy our work. However, authors cannot depend on people submitting feedback and comments regarding the site. We need to be more intentional and proactive.

First of all, make use of statistical plug-ins for your website. We suggest WPStats or RankMath SEO. These transparently collect vital data 24/7, revealing how many people visit your site, which pages they visit, and how long they stay. This is the beginning point of developing a better understanding of how people use your site.

In addition, consider using formal or informal questions, surveys, or market research, to determine the needs and preferences of your site visitors.

Return to the many different features available through WordPress, such as widgets, plug-ins, and add-ons. Determine what is within your reach and may be beneficial for your users to fully understand your message.

We list examples of specific plug-ins that may be helpful below. All of these are also listed in Chapter 10 and our companion resource page at https://writingworkswonders.com/author-resources/website-creation-for-authors/ .

Recommended Plugins for Content Support

Broken Link Checker

* Link Checker

Button Maker (Accessible buttons)

* MaxButtons

Form Makers

* Ninja Forms

* WPForms

* MailerLite Form plug-in for MailerLite system

* MailChimp plug-in for MailChimp system

Payment Processing

* WP Easy PayPal

Payment Accept

* WP PayPal

Podcasting

* Pinecast WordPress Sync

* WP RSS Aggregator Security

* WordFence Security

Social Media

* Social Media Follow Buttons Bar

Social Media Display/Integration

* There are many plug-ins available in this category.

Securing Feedback

We mentioned feedback from users. Consider these basic questions as you delve into this area.

- Will a feedback form be sufficient for my needs? (It's an excellent starting point!.)
- What are other ways I might conveniently conduct market research?

We know that very few people use the feedback form or Contact Us form on websites. We're lucky if they use them if they have a problem! Other than that, generally, people won't send comments via our websites. At least among our followers, we find that a greater number of visitors will click an email address and send us a direct email message instead. (This hesitancy to use forms maybe higher in our community of individuals with visual impairment because forms often are not accessible to users of screen readers. Even though our forms are screen reader compatible, visitors hesitate to use them.)

Therefore, to gather a broader base of input for your market research, you may need to reach out further.

Here are some strategies Kathy has used over the years with success.

- Assemble focus groups to review your site (make sure they span the demographics of your target audience). Gentle warning do not just invite your friends or relatives!

- Invite your local author or writing group to provide their feedback. Send them an online feedback form and offer to include those who complete it in a drawing!
- Present a five-minute guided tour – In person or via Zoom provide an overview of your site to your writing group and ask for their immediate verbal feedback. (Record the session, to ensure you capture all their responses.)
- Use data from your website and emails! Choose a mailing list program for marketing that enables you to see how many people are actually reading the emails that you send and click the links in them.

- Continue to read articles about website design and marketing for authors.

Market research can take so many shapes and forms. It includes thinking about interacting with people who regularly visit our website or would be potential visitors to our website.

- Where are those potential visitors?
- What is happening in those spaces?
- How can you participate and share your message and website information?

For instance, Cheryl has done a great deal of work making sure that Writing Works Wonders is visible on social media. From Facebook to Twitter, LinkedIn, Instagram, and beyond, she shares information about our events and new releases regularly.

Another strategy is continuing to review the changes to author websites and other materials produced by authors like you. Subscribe to their mailing list to see what they're using for promotions. Would any of those fit your genre, theme, and budget?

Final Thoughts

Use the same strategy we used in this book of gradual involvement. Do not invest “whole hog” with time and effort but test the waters to see if you like it, is it feasible, and what your "return on investment" will likely be.

Using data in decision making, whether it's how many people visit the site, buy your books, or listen to your podcast, helps you understand your audience. Sort and evaluate the data you collect to see the impact of actions or changes you make. These are some ways you may determine the best use of your resources and time.

Follow-Up Questions Chapter Eight

1. What are your initial plans for how you will collect feedback about your site?
2. How frequently will you collect feedback?
3. What do you expect will be further stages of development for your site?

4. Which additional features would you like to include? List them and then prioritize them, 1 being the most important.
5. Which sources should you watch for trends and development in your genre? Are there specific authors, publications, or websites you should track or can you subscribe to their mailing lists?

CHAPTER NINE
What's Next

There are many additional features that you may add to your website over time. Fortunately, WordPress has most of these features either built into it or integrated through plug-ins which we've already demonstrated are very easy to install. Following is a list of some of the major features you might consider in the future once you've established your site. We discuss each suggestion briefly.

- Mailing list
- Newsletter
- Social Media feeds
- Blog
- Podcast

MAILING LIST

A mailing list can be easily developed by using a contact form on your website to collect addresses rather than posting your email address. Contact form plug-ins include WP Form, Ninja Form, and many others.

However, also consider that you may want to use a full-blown mailing list platform. The huge benefits are several, but here are a few that will really please you. First, these mailing list programs instantly import the information your visitors input on your site into the mailing list platform. Second, they allow you to design professional-looking mailings. Third, these systems allow you to monitor and track your mailing list. Finally, there are at least two platforms that have decent, free capacities available and excellent WordPress plug-in integrations: MailerLite.com and MailChimp.com.

Newsletter

Eventually, your occasional emails may turn into more formal newsletters. If you choose a robust mailing program such as those listed above, you can use that same platform to design and send these newsletters to your email list.

Success!

Social Media Feeds

Most professionals spend time on social media to increase their visibility and brand in the public eye and be part of the conversation. Isn't it brilliant when we can do one activity and have it serve more than one purpose?

Here is one of those brilliant solutions! Social media feeds to connect with social media plug-ins. Install the plug-in, configure, and then add the widget to your sidebar. Now whatever you most recently posted on the designated social media account will appear in that section of the sidebar. As you post to Facebook or Twitter, the widget updates your information for you! (I know it seems like it is magic, but honestly it's a social media feed.)

For more information about social media posting for authors, listen to

Episode 10 of Writing Works Wonders! We had a terrific discussion with Seamus King on this topic.

Social Media for Authors Episode 10 https://writingworkswonders.com/2021/06/06/ep-10-writing-works-wonders-advancing-beyond-barriers/

Blogging

If you decide you want to add a blog to your site, this section reveals how to start, post, choose your blog page, and add it to your menu.

As you might have gathered from the prior chapters, blogging is the name for presenting information in a serial or sequential manner to your website readers.

Sample Blog Topics for Authors

- Updates about your writing
- Upcoming publications
- Future speaking engagements
- Extra material for your books – unpublished scenes or chapters
- Your life/ memoire related material
- Insights about the writing craft
- Answers to fan mail
- Your own podcast
- Your interviews
- Endless other possibilities

STARTING A BLOG

Use the list above as a beginning **point to consider ideas for your author blog. Evaluate whether you have time to write a paragraph or**

two once a week or once a month. Determine whether there would be sufficient added value to pursue a blog at this time versus investing your energy in other endeavors.

If your evaluation is that a blog on a specific topic, or two, is a good idea right now, move ahead. If not, wait until it is, if ever. There is no rule saying you have to blog. Oh yeah, who is Master of the Universe?

Posting to Your Blog

Once you have selected your topic/s, this is probably the easiest part! To post, draft your content in a word processor, grammar- and spell-check it.

* Go to WordPress Dashboard.

* Click Post.
* Click Add New.
* Fill in a title for your blog post.
* Add the content.
* Select Categories/Tags that might link together many of your posts.
* Click Publish.

Your blog post will automatically show up in the blog feed which is part of your theme. If it is not, you can add the main blog page to your menu and then set up a widget to add all posts with the same assigned category.

First-time Blog Setup Summary

- Create a dedicated page where all your blog posts will appear in order.
- Go to Dashboard

- Pages
- New Page
- Name it Blog or Newsletter
- Publish the page!
- Return to Dashboard
- Click Settings
- Then Reading
- Skip Home Page. Options, If you want the blog page as your home page you can click among the first options.
- Go to "Posts page." As authors, we usually just want to identify the blog page at this point.
- So, click "Posts Page" and in that combination box, select the Page you just created (our example was Blog or Newsletter).
- There are several options to review.

- One we suggest changing is “For each post in the feed, include.” At this point, instead of “Full text,” select “Excerpt or Summary.” This option reduces the length of the blog page and inserts a “Read more” link after the excerpt for your post entry.
- Then click “Save Changes.”
- Once you add your blog page to your menu, you are up and running!

Blog Posting Summary

Dashboard

Click Posts

— Add New

—— Enter Content

——— Select or Add Categories or Tags

——— Click Publish

PODCAST

Perhaps you already have a podcast that you host or co-host. There are great ways to integrate it into your website as well so that the most recent content will display.

There are several widgets and media player HTML code snippets that can be used to display existing podcast feeds in your sidebar or on a dedicated web page.

We recommend Pinecast as a highly accessible and very helpful podcast hosting service. If you are beginning a new podcast account with Pinecast, there is a wonderful WordPress plug-in, so visitors will have easy access right on your site. If you are new to Pinecast or upgrading, we have a discount code just for you.

Go to pinecast.com and enter the code, WRITING.

You will receive forty percent (40%) off your first three months on a new account, or if you upgrade your current Pinecast account.

The Pinecast plug-in is truly awesome. Once configured, every time you post a new podcast episode, the plugin pulls the audio and description content into your website, creating a new audio-blog style post! Instant content transfer. Sweet!

In addition, Pinecast, like many major podcast hosts, provides a customizable media player. This means once you have your podcast up and running, you can choose colors and dimensions for your online player. Then you just copy the code into the HTML side of WordPress. And bingo! You have a classy-looking and accessible player that updates instantly every time you upload new content. Look Mom, no hands!

Visit www.WritingWorksWonders.com we have this media player over in the right sidebar and on a dedicated page, currently named “Click and Play.”

MORE CONTENT FEATURES FOR AUTHORS

Consider also how you might be able to import or integrate content from book review sites such as GoodReads.com, Amazon.com, and Smashwords.com into your site. These might be imported into a sidebar widget or a dedicated page. Your choice!

Furthermore, what about your publishing house? Do they have information you can link to or import? Do you want to include their logo on your site? Also contact them so they list your website URL, wherever your author information is listed.

EXPLORE

When we say "Explore," we are encouraging you to consider new opportunities to incorporate or directly feed content from your publisher or if you are an independently published author from your distribution points such as Smashwords, Draft2Digital, Kindle Direct Publishing, Audible, and other places current and future readers may discover for your work!

For more details about publishing with Smashwords and Kindle Direct, listen to the following episodes of Writing Works Wonders.

Smashwords.com Episode 32 https://writingworkswonders.com/2021/10/17/ep-32-writing-works-wonders/

Kindle Direct Publishing Episode 11. https://writingworkswonders.com/2021/06/09/ep-11-writing-works-wonders/

Watch the Writing Works Wonders and podcast feed as we will be posting a new podcast with Draft2Digital later in 2022!

CONGRATULATIONS!

This is the finish line, friends. You have read through the entire instructions on how to make the choices and set up your own WordPress author website. And no doubt others besides authors have joined us along the journey as well!

You have a roadmap for designing your site. You have exercises and steps to walk you through the journey. And you know it, you are Master of the Universe.

The decisions are yours to make. Web site development is another opportunity to share your creativity. Most importantly, it is a way to share your message with the world. As we mentioned before, creating your own site provides you with the ultimate control over that message.

We hope this book, and the companion podcast episodes, provide an inspiring and effective resource for your website work. Please reach out to us. We want to know how you are faring and what great work you create!

Remember, it does not have to be perfect. Your site is always a work in progress, just like each one of us! Happy Writing!

CHAPTER TEN
Online Resources

In addition to this short book, we have a two-part podcast series on website design for authors. Like this book, the podcast episodes are focused on the needs of those with visual impairment. Following is the main link to not only these two episodes but also all the resources mentioned in this book and more. It is intended to be an evergreen resource to which we continue to add new discoveries and update those which may become outdated. That's not always possible with a book, even an ebook.

Book and Podcast Resource Page

https://writingworkswonders.com/author-resources/website-creation-for-authors/

Website Design for Authors

Podcast Episodes & Resources

Two-Part Podcast Series

This Website Design for Author's two-part podcast series is a special production of Writing Works Wonders for our listeners and authors. What do authors need to know about website development? Dr. Kathy King is center stage and uses her nearly 20 years of website design and publishing experience to guide our authors through the process. Kathy provides recommended development stages, platforms, and steps to follow. And Cheryl makes sure she explains the technical aspects and keeps it all in perspective!

Episode 45 Podcast Resources

Hosting (Server space to install website)

- HostGator
- GoDaddy
- DreamHost

URL Purchasing – Buy your web address

- HostGator
- GoDaddy

Website Platforms

- WordPress – Recommended
- Wix
- Squarespace

- HostGator- Many options
- GoDaddy- Many options

WordPress Themes

- GeneratePress is a highly accessible theme for website creators and users. As of the date of publication, Generate Press is free. Please note, if you find it beneficial, you may consider supporting the developer with a donation or upgrading to the premium version for more features.
- Through the WordPress dashboard, you may review thousands of themes. Many may be optimized for greater accessibility with custom design and plugins.

ACCESSIBILITY GUIDELINES

- WCAG – Web Content Accessibility Guidelines – Recommendations to support compliance with ADA requirements for web accessibility
- W3.org – Provides complete information for individuals planning and designing websites
- Create an Accessibility Policy- Use this free tool to generate an Accessibility Policy/Statement for your website.

Recommended Plug-ins for WordPress

- Accessibility
    - One-Click Accessibility
    - Accessibility Tool and Alt Text Finder

    - W3.org- Accessibility Guidelines- (Not a plugin)
- Backup
    - UpDraftPlus Backup/Restore
- Broken Link Checker
    - Link Checker
- Button Maker (Accessible buttons)
    - MaxButtons
- Form Makers
    - Ninja Forms
    - WPForms
    - MailerLite Form plugin for MailerLite system
    - MailChimp plugin for MailChimp system
- Payment Processing
    - WP Easy PayPal Payment Accept
    - WP PayPal

- Podcasting
    - Pinecast WordPress Sync
    - WP RSS Aggregator
- Security
    - WordFence Security
- Social Media
    - Social Media Follow Buttons Bar
- Statistics
    - Rank Math SEO
    - WPStats

Website How - To - Books/Articles

- Writing Works Wonders' website design for authors book- This book!!
- 5 Things Author's Websites Need for Success

APPENDIX A
JAWS/ NVDA
Keystrokes

JAWS SCREEN READER

Web Browsing Keystrokes for Jaws
From Freedom Scientific
https://support.freedomscientific.com/Content/Documents/Manuals/JAWS/Keystrokes.pdf

FUSION

If you have low vision, you may be interested in Fusion, also located at the above web link. Fusion combines magnification with JAWS. You can use them together or choose to use them separately.

NVDAccess (NVDA) Free Screen Reader

Go to the link below to access the up-to-date download NVDA information. The American Foundation for the Blind provides downloads in pdf and audio (mp3) format.

https://www.afb.org/blindness-and-low-vision/using-technology/assistive-technology-videos/learn-nvda

Appendix B
iOS VoiceOver

How to access VoiceOver on your IOS device

Settings

— Accessibility

—— VoiceOver

Explore! You will see "VoiceOver Practice." Take advantage of this feature to learn VoiceOver.

1. SPEECH

1. **VOICE**: Choose the voice you prefer.
2. **SPEAKING RATE**: Adjust the speed VoiceOver reads.
3. **PITCH:** Adjust voice Pitch.
4. **DETECT LANGUAGE:** Toggle on/off. When On, VoiceOver

detects and reads different languages.

2. **BRAILLE**: If you are using a Braille device to input or read from your device, tap here.

3. **VOICEOVER RECOGNITION:** You may think you need this on, however we recommend you do not turn on if you are planning on using voiceover. It will cause conflicts in certain apps and websites.

4. **VERBOSITY:** How do you want Voiceover to read your text? Do you want to hear every punctuation mark, some, or none at all? You can also choose to hear or not to hear all hints read aloud to you.

5. **AUDIO:** This option is for people using external audio devices.

6. **COMMANDS:** Touch Gestures may become your best friend! We suggest

That you find "2-finger swipe," and change it to "Next Rotor."

Change 2-finger swipe right to "Previous Rotor." (You can always change it back if you don't like it!) The default is set to take two fingers, double-tap and hold on the second tap, then rotate your hand to find the Rotor option you want.

7. **ACTIVITIES:** Allows you to change a group of commands when using the rotor or in an app.

8. **ROTOR:** This is the place that you get to choose what you want in your Rotor. Think of your Rotor as a place for shortcuts. There are too many to list. Look around and remember that you can put them in and then you can take them out. You have choices!

9: **ROTOR ACTIONS:** We do not claim to be the experts. Cheryl is an Apple Teacher, but we recommend that you explore it yourself. If you have a problem with an app while it is on, go back to settings and turn it off. Restart your device. If you still have an issue, then you'll know that it wasn't this setting.

10. **TYPING:** This is where you choose how you want Voiceover to read what you type: letter, word, or wait to read sentence?

11: QUICK SETTINGS: Choose the settings that you want to be accessible quickly with a tap or swipe.

12: **NAVIGATION STYLES**: Choose your preference - flat or grouped.

13. **NAVIGATE IMAGES**: This allows you to place your finger on an image and it will tell you what you are looking at. A person, a dog, a tree... Once you have faces labeled in your photo app, it will speak the person's name.

14. **LARGE CURSOR:** Speaks for itself.

15. **CAPTION PANEL:** On or off.

16. **DOUBLE TAP TIME OUT:** The default is "three-finger double-tap." While Voiceover is on, you can double-tap with three fingers and it will turn Voiceover off until you do another three-finger double-tap.

Go to the link below for more accessibility options and how to use them.

APPENDIX C
Accessible Submenus

This section is in the appendix because you will not need it unless you create submenus. Here are the steps to create Jaws (and NVDA) accessible submenus.

Once you have several items in your menu and you want to move a few items into a submenu, follow these steps.

For our illustration, we have not published our third book. We want to create a main menu item Books and submenu items book 1, book 2, and book 3.

Summary Steps

Submenu Creation

- Go to WordPress Dashboard
- Click on "Appearance"
- Click "Menus"
- In the left box, "Add Menu Items"
- Click on "Custom Links"
- In the "URL" box type "#" (Yes, the hashtag key and that's all.)
- In the "Link Text" box, type "Books"
- Click "Add to Menu"
- Now in the right-hand box, "Menu Structure" you will see your Books menu item at the bottom of the list.
- Move it to the spot you want it as you did before with menu items.
- Click "Save Menu"
- Now move the web pages listed as Books 1, 2, and 3 to the spots right below "Books"
- Then flick each of these open and click "Move under Books."
- Click "Save Menu"

Made in the USA
Monee, IL
05 November 2026

67381969R00115